The Little Muslim Book Of Al-Isrā' & Al-Mi'rāj

الإسراء والمعراج

A GREEN FIG BOOK

Green Fig

Designed by

CHY Illustration & Design

Name:

Publisher: Green Fig
Pennsylvania, USA
www.gogreenfig.com

Green Fig
Proud Muslim Kids

Dear Parents & Teachers

We are excited to bring to your children the story of al-Isrā' (The Night Journey) & al-Mi'rāj (The Ascension). God sent the prophets as a mercy to us, and supported them with miracles that indicate the truthfulness of their message. Of all the Prophets, our Prophet Muḥammad was blessed with the most miracles, the greatest of which is the Qur'ān. Al-Isrā' and al-Mi'rāj is a great miracle of Prophet Muḥammad. It was a physical journey by body and soul and took only part of one night. It occurred before the Prophet migrated to al-Madinah. Al-Isrā' and al-Mi'rāj is commemorated on the 27th of Rajab, though there are different sayings for the scholars about the exact date of this miracle. When reading *The Little Muslim Book of Al-Isrā' & Al-Mi'rāj*, your child is set to embark in an amazing journey of knowledge because of the many precious lessons present in this glorious miracle.

We will be happy to hear from you info@gogreenfig.com

Green Fig Staff

Introduction

Al-Isrā' and al-Mi'rāj (the Night Journey and the Ascension), is a great miracle of Prophet Muḥammad (ﷺ محمّد). Al-Isrā' is the night journey from Makkah to Jerusalem, and al-Mi'rāj is the ascension of the Prophet to the upper world. They both happened during the night of the 27th of Rajab, before the Prophet migrated to al-Madinah.

Prophet Muhammad was staying in the house of his cousin Umm Hāni' in Makkah. He was sleeping with his uncle Hamzah on one side, and his cousin Ja'far on the other.

The ceiling of the house opened, and Angel Jibril (Gabriel), the best angel, descended. He awakened the Prophet to take him on this honorable and magnificent journey.

The Night Journey Al-Isrā'

Al Aqsā Mosque

Makkah

From Masjid al-Ḥarām, Jibril and our Prophet rode al-Burāq, an extraordinary animal from Paradise. Al-Burāq is beautiful and white in color. It is bigger than a donkey but smaller than a mule. It has wings and is super-fast. When it comes to a high place, its back legs elongate; and when it comes to a low place, its front legs elongate.

The Buraq set forth placing its hoof where its sight reached until they arrived in a land with palm trees. The Prophet dismounted and prayed. This was al-Madinah, the city that our Prophet later migrated to.

The Burāq continued with the Prophet riding behind Jibril until they reached a whitish land. The Prophet dismounted and prayed. This was Madyan, the city of Prophet Shu'ayb.

The Burāq continued with the Prophet riding behind Jibril until they reached another land. The Prophet dismounted and prayed. This was Mount Sinai (Tur Sina'), where Prophet Moses received the revelation from God.

The Burāq continued with the Prophet riding behind Jibril until they reached a land where they could see its palaces. The Prophet dismounted and prayed. This was Bethlehem (Bayt Laḥm), where Prophet Jesus was born.

Then the Burāq took off with our Prophet and Jibril until they entered the city of Jerusalem. It is in this blessed land, that al-Aqsā mosque (Masjid al-Aqsā), an old mosque, first built by Prophet Adam, is located.

The Prophet entered this mosque and saw all the Prophets, from Adam to Jesus, may peace be upon them, gathered. Our Prophet led them in prayer. All the prophets came with one religion—the religion of Islam—the only true religion. The prophets are the best of the creations, and the best among them is Muhammad, the last Prophet.

During The Journey From Makkah To Jerusalem, The Prophet Saw Many Great Signs.

Among what he saw:

* The Prophet saw the world (dunyā) in the image of an old woman. This tells us that what has passed from this world is much more than what remains.

* The Prophet saw a bull coming out from a very small opening, then was trying in vain to return through it. Jibril told the Prophet,"This is the example of the bad word~once spoken, it cannot be taken back."

The Prophet smelled a very nice scent coming from a grave. Jibril told him it was the grave of the woman who used to comb and style Pharoah's daughter hair. This woman was a very good Muslim. One day, as she was combing Pharaoh's daughter's hair, the comb fell from her hand. As she was picking it up, she said, "Bismillāh", which means in the name of God. At that, Pharaoh's daughter asked her, "Do you have a god other than my father?" The woman said," My Lord

and the Lord of your father is Allāh."
Pharaoh ordered the woman to leave
Islam and threatened her he would
kill her and her children if she did not.
She stayed strong and refused to
blaspheme. So Pharoah started to
throw her children one by one into a
huge cauldron of boiling water. When
he was about to take her youngest
child—a little boy still nursing—God
enabled this child to speak. He said,

"O mother, be patient. The torture of the Hereafter is far more severe than the torture of this world. Do not waver, because you are right." At that, she asked Pharaoh to bury her bones and her children's in the same grave. She died with her children as martyrs. In the Hereafter, she will be with them in Paradise where they will live happily forever.

The Ascension -Al-Mi'rāj

From al-Aqsā Mosque, the Prophet ascended to the upper world. Above us there are seven heavens full of angels. Heavens are the place where angels live. The first heaven is that blue thing we see when we look up and there are no clouds. The Prophet ascended to the heavens on extraordinary stairs that we don't see, called al-Mirqat, with alternating steps of gold and silver.

When the Prophet and Jibril arrived at the first heaven, Jibril asked the angel in charge to open the door, and Prophet Muhammad entered the first heaven. Our Prophet ascended with Jibril to each of the seven heavens.

In the first
He saw Prophet Adam.

In the second he saw
Prophets Jesus (ʿĪsā) and John (Yaḥyā).

In the third
He saw Prophet Joseph (Yūsuf).

In the fourth
He saw Prophet Enoch (Idrīs).

In the fifth
He saw Prophet Aaron (Hārūn).

In the sixth
He saw Prophet Moses (Mūsā).

In the seventh
He saw Prophet Abraham (Ibrahīm)..

In the seventh heaven, our Prophet saw al-Bayt al-Ma'mūr. Al-Bayt al-Ma'mūr to the angels is like the Ka'bah to us. Every day, 70,000 angels enter it, pray, then leave, and never return to it. This shows how great the number of the angels is. It is more than the numbers of the grains of the sand on the beaches and the leaves of the trees.

In the seventh heaven, our Prophet saw also Sidrat al-Muntahā. This is a huge tree; its roots are in the sixth heaven and it extends past the seventh. Its fruits are as big as large water jars. Its leaves are the size of elephant ears. It is visited by golden butterflies. When these butterflies gather on Sidrat al-Muntahā, no creation can describe its beauty.

At Sidrat al-Muntahā, Jibril got very close to our Prophet. There, the Prophet saw Angel Jibril in his original angelic form with 600 wings. Each of his wings is so big that it fills the entire horizon.

Then the Prophet ascended to Paradise above the seventh heaven. The Prophet entered Paradise, the abode of everlasting happiness for the believers, and saw some of the enjoyments God prepared for them.

Among what he saw are the *wildānul-mukhalladūn* who are created to serve the inhabitants of Paradise in the Hereafter. The least in status in Paradise will have 10,000 of them to serve him. Each one of them would carry a tray of gold in one hand and a tray of silver in the other hand.

The Prophet saw **The Throne (al-'Arsh)**, which is the ceiling of Paradise.

The Throne is the largest creation in size; God did not create anything bigger than it. The Throne compared to the seven heavens and the earth is like the ocean compared to a drop of water. God created the Throne as a sign of His Power and He did not create the Throne to sit on it. God is not a body and God does not need any place. God does not need anything.

Then the Prophet ascended beyond Paradise. He reached a place where he heard the creaking of the pens used by the angels who are copying from the Guarded Tablet. This Tablet is in the form of one giant pearl surrounded with rubies. Everything that happens until the Day of Judgement is written in the Guarded Tablet.

On this blessed night, God revealed to our Prophet the obligation of the five prayers.

The Prophet Returns To Makkah

After the Ascension, the Prophet returned to Makkah. It was still night. The next day, the Prophet told the people what happened to him the previous night.

The non-believers belied the Prophet and mocked him, saying, "We need a month to go to Jerusalem and come back, and you are claiming to have done all this in one night?" They said to Abu Bakr, "Look at what your companion is saying."

Abu Bakr told them, "If he said that, then he is truthful. From that incident, Abu Bakr was called "as-Siddiq" because of how strongly he believed all what the Prophet said.

الصِّدِّيق

The non-believers questioned the Prophet: "If you are truthful, then describe al-Aqsā Mosque to us." God enabled our Prophet to see al-Aqsā Mosque in front of him. He described the mosque and its surroundings in perfect detail.

Although these
non-believers admitted
that the Prophet's
description was exact, they
did not believe in him and
become Muslim.

Conclusion

The ascension was a miracle to honor Prophet Muhammad, may peace be upon him, by seeing the wonders of the upper world.

The reason for that trip was not to go where God is, because God does not occupy any place. God is not in the heavens, nor on the throne, nor on earth. God existed before He created all places.

We glorify God, The Exalted, from attributing to him any attributes of the creations.

We thank God for giving our Prophet the great miracle of al-Isrā' and al-Miʻrāj.

Al-Isrā' & Al-Mi'rāj is a miracle of Prophet Muḥammad.

Al-Isrā' is the night journey of Prophet Muḥammad from Makkah to al-Aqsā Mosque in Jerusalem.

Al-Mi'rāj is the ascension of Prophet Muḥammad to the upper world.

All Prophets are Muslims.

Prophet Adam is the first Prophet.

Prophet Muḥammad is the last and best Prophet.

A bad world is harmful.

We are winners if we are patient and remain steadfast on Islam.

There are seven heavens or skies.

Heavens are solid bodies with doors.

The heavens are where angels live.

All angels are good Muslims.

The best angel is Jibril (Gabriel).

Paradise is above the seventh heaven.

Paradise is the abode of everlasting happiness for the believers.

The Throne is the biggest creation in size.

The Throne is the ceiling of Paradise.

God is not in heavens nor on the Throne.

God is not a body. God does not occupy any place.

Encourage Your Child To Memorize

God said in the Qur'ān in Sūrat al-Isrā' , verse 1:

﴿سُبْحَانَ الَّذِي أَسْرَى بِعَبْدِهِ لَيْلاً مِّنَ الْمَسْجِدِ الْحَرَامِ إِلَى الْمَسْجِدِ الأَقْصَى الَّذِي بَارَكْنَا حَوْلَهُ لِنُرِيَهُ مِنْ آياتِنَآ إِنَّهُ هُوَ السَّمِيعُ البَصِيرُ﴾

Which means:

"Praise be to God Who enabled His slave, Mu<u>h</u>ammad,

to make the journey at night from Masjid al-<u>H</u>arām

in Makkah to Masjid al-Aqsā in Jerusalem, which is

surrounded by a blessed land."

The Proud Muslim Kids series by Green Fig is designed to engagingly teach youngsters basic concepts of Islam in a way that speaks to their hearts and minds. Each book in the series is crafted by a staff of qualified educators, writers, illustrators, parents and children. Not only is the Proud Muslim Kids series designed to supplement the early childhood and elementary Islamic curriculum, it is a great addition to any school or home library. Covering a wide variety of topics such as the Five Pillars of Islam, Islamic culture, and Islamic history, parents and children will return to these books and enjoy them together time and time again.